Praying for the Dead

Revd Dr Meg Gilley

**The Churches' Fellowship for
Psychical and Spiritual Studies**

2023

This first edition was published in 2023, by:
The Churches' Fellowship for Psychical and Spiritual Studies
The Creative Suite, Mill 3, Pleasley Vale Business Park
Mansfield, NG19 8RL

Email: gensec@churchesfellowship.co.uk
www.churchesfellowship.co.uk

ISBN: 0 902666 51 7

Printed by
East Coast Grafix, LN11 7LN

Contents

1

Acknowledgements

Though this project began as a personal endeavour, it quickly drew in the interest and assistance of many others, all of whom have contributed ideas and suggestions, pointed to other sources, and read early drafts. The work is much richer for all that they have brought.

Within the CFPSS, Santha Bhattacharji and Ellen Davis helped guide the project all the way through. Many others made suggestions, including John Wyborn, Andrew Cort, and Matt Arnold.

Other friends also assisted: Michael Keeling, Brian Elliott and Ian Gomersall.

And many others, who were kind enough to listen and respond.

I am grateful to them all.

I recognise that this is a work in progress. It doesn't offer the last word on the subject, but takes a tentative step in exploring an important topic. There is much still to do!

Meg Gilley
August 2023

Praying for the Dead: A Personal Introduction
- How We Got Here

I retired from my parish where I served as an Anglican priest a month after the first Covid lockdown began in 2020, without fuss or farewells, plunged into a silent, separate world. It was brilliant. I loved lockdown. My husband and I went for walks and discovered new places all around County Durham. And I read and prayed and waited for God to tell me who I was in this new stage of my life, who God was for me, and what my service would be now. There was no immediate answer, in fact, no answer at all for a long while.

I began to be more involved with the CFPSS. I had been a member for 20 years, paid my subs and skim-read the magazines, and attended one conference. In lockdown, when we weren't allowed in church, the CFPSS became my church community – attending Zoom Mass during Lent, and the Thursday evening discussion group on WhatsApp.

As a parish priest, I felt that my mission was set out in the Benedictus which I said every day – to "go before the Lord to prepare his way, to give his people the knowledge of salvation by the forgiveness of their sins", especially in our work with asylum seekers through Bible Study and preparation for baptism.

Gradually, I discovered that my role in retirement was also set out in the Benedictus : "to shine on those who dwell in darkness and the shadow of death". I came to experience a vocation to pray for the dead. I am still working out what that means for me, and this booklet of prayers is part of that exploration.

The booklet envisages a group of people praying together – either physically present with each other or remotely through electronic means – and praying for those who have left this earthly life. It can also be used by a person praying alone if necessary, but the mutual support of a group is preferable. The theological introduction sets out what I have come to understand about praying for the dead. I still have a lot to learn.

I invite you to take part in this work. If this booklet sparks an interest, maybe you share this calling?

The Revd Dr Meg Gilley

Praying for the Dead: A Theological Reflection

Praying for loved ones who have died is almost instinctual. People want to remember them and to ask God to take care of them. Though the Church of England advises us to *remember* the dead before the Lord, we often hear church intercessors talking explicitly in terms of *praying for* those who have left this life.

This booklet is for those who feel especially called to pray systematically for those who have passed over from their life on earth. It envisages a group of pray-ers praying together or remotely for those who have died recently, those whose anniversaries occur, and those who have lost their lives suddenly or tragically. Prayers are also included for those whose lives on earth were not healthy or wholesome and who caused great harm to others.

We recognise that this will be anathema to some. Since the Reformation, praying for the dead has been controversial in the Anglican church in Britain. Some people believe that at the point of death your condition is fixed and cannot be changed by the prayers of the living. The antipathy to prayers for the dead arose, at least in part, as a reaction against the concept of purgatory, and the abuses associated with this in the Middle Ages, such as charging for indulgences, pardons and prayers for the dead, to reduce the time spent in purgatory. This is reflected in Article 22 of the Articles of Religion of the Anglican Church:

> The Romish Doctrine concerning Purgatory, Pardons, Worshipping and Adoration, as well of Images as of Reliques, and also Invocation of Saints, is a fond thing vainly invented, and grounded upon no warranty of Scripture, but rather repugnant to the Word of God.

For others, on the other hand, praying for the dead expresses "a simple, trustful confidence in the loving care and mercy of a heavenly Father ... [who] will do more either than they desire or deserve."[1]

---

[1] Archbishops' Commission on Christian Doctrine, *Prayer and the Departed*, p. 19.

The Bible and Theology

Underlying this controversy is what we believe about life after death and beyond. Ultimately, the Bible says, we will all be raised at the bodily resurrection. Between death and the final resurrection is an intermediate state, which Paul calls "sleep" (1 Cor 7:39, 11:30, 15:6, 18, 20, 51). N T Wright describes this as a state of "restful happiness",[2] incorporating all those who have died in Christ. The state of sleep might be (i) conscious, a time of sanctification or glorification; (ii) unconscious; or (iii) a mythological idea, because the faithful dead have already reached the fullness of salvation.[3]

Where does this traditional eschatological pattern of death leave us in praying for the dead?

The Report of the Archbishops' Commission on Christian Doctrine (1971) says:

> The whole Commission acknowledges that any prayer for the dead which is to gain full acceptance in the Church of England must speak only in terms of those themes which are central in the witness of Scripture, for example, our incorporation in Christ crucified and risen, our share in the first-fruits of the Holy Spirit, and our expectation of the consummation of all things at the Last Day. Some of the members of the Commission are persuaded .... That it is only proper to pray by name for the living and that prayers for the dead, if they are to be made at all, must not be offered by name, but be cast in general terms.[4]

The Commission reached a compromise in the form of words that might be used in churches without controversy:

> We thank thee, O God, for the life and witness of thy servant N., whom we remember before you this day.[5]

---

[2] Wright, *For All the Saints?*, p. 36.
[3] Cocksworth, *Prayer and the Departed*, pp. 13-16. See also Archbishops' Commission on Christian Doctrine, *Prayer and the Departed*, p. 43 section 38.
[4] Archbishops' Commission on Christian Doctrine, *Prayer and the Departed*, p.46 section 44.
[5] Archbishops' Commission on Christian Doctrine, *Prayer and the Departed*, p. 52 section 60.

In other words, to remember someone before God or commend them to God was acceptable, but to pray for them was not.

Christopher Cocksworth (1997) suggests three principles: (i) The faithful dead do not need our prayers to thrive in the afterlife; (ii) we should affirm that the faithful departed are in Christ; and (iii) our prayers should recognise that "the fullness of salvation is still to come for the dead as well as the living".[6]

N T Wright says, "True prayer is an outflowing of love; if I love someone, I will want to pray for them, not necessarily because they are in difficulties, not necessarily because there is a particular need of which I'm aware, but simply because holding them up in God's presence is the most natural and appropriate thing to do, and because I believe that God chooses to work through our prayers for other people's benefit, whatever sort of benefit that may be. ... there is no reason at all why love should discontinue the practice of holding the beloved in prayer before God."[7] Wright goes on to tell the story of Professor Sir Norman Anderson, whose three children had all died in early adult life. He prayed for them all because he wanted to talk to God about them and share his love for them with God who made them and loved them.

The Bible itself does not advocate praying for the dead. Nor does it forbid it. There are examples of prayers for the dead in the Hebrew Bible (eg 1 Kings 17:20-22), intertestamental literature (eg 2 Maccabees 12:39-45) and the New Testament,[8] including Jesus praying for his dead friend Lazarus (John 11:41-44) and Peter praying for Tabitha (Acts 9:40-41).

There is evidence that Christians prayed for the dead from the mid-second century,[9] as recorded on tombstones in the catacombs, and in the writings of Tertullian, Augustine, John Chrysostom and many others. *The Passion of Perpetua and Felicitas* tells of Perpetua, whose deceased brother appears to her in a dream as disfigured and suffering from a dreadful disease.

---

[6] Cocksworth, *Prayer and the Departed*, p. 17
[7] Wright, *For All the Saints?*, pp. 73-74.
[8] See the first article on this subject in Matt Arnold's website "Praying for the Dead? What Does this Mean?" (ghostghoulsandgod.co.uk)
[9] See Matt Arnold's second article in the series "Praying for the Dead: Early Christian Beliefs - Ghosts, Ghouls and God" (ghostsghoulsandgod.co.uk)

After praying regularly for him, he appears in her dreams again, this time radiant and restored.

So praying for the dead was practised regularly until the Reformation. Luther discouraged the contemporary practice of holding Masses and vigils for the dead, and advised that one or two prayers that God's will might be done for the deceased were acceptable, but nothing more.[10] His views changed the attitude of the Protestant world to praying for the dead, and influenced Anglican approaches.

The Orthodox and Catholic churches continue to pray for the dead today. The Catholic doctrine assumes an intermediate state of purgatory, where souls at death are purified, with the aid of the prayers of those still on earth "so as to achieve the holiness necessary to enter the joy of heaven".[11]

Praying for the Dead in Contemporary Anglican Liturgy

This expression of theology is reflected in prayers for the dead in contemporary Church of England liturgy. The intercessions in the Eucharist in Common Worship generally include the opportunity to pray about those who have died. They are remembered and commended to God's keeping, but for the most part no specific requests are actually made on their behalf. These prayers are characterised by references to the communion of saints and the kingdom of heaven. The emphasis is on the faithful dead, including those whose faith is known to God alone. Those of no faith or of other faiths or of semi-faith are not mentioned. Those who pray are not asking God to do anything other than fulfil His promises. They are not asking God to deviate from his original intentions. When these prayers are offered in church, it is customary to name those who have died recently and those whose anniversaries fall at the time.

> "We remember those who have gone before us in the peace of Christ, and we give you praise for all your faithful ones, with whom we rejoice in the communion of saints." [12]

---

[10] Luther on Prayer for the Dead and Communicating with Spirits (cph.org)
[11] *Catechism of the Catholic Church*, para 1030 – 1032, p 235
[12] Archbishops' Council, *Common Worship*, p. 281

"And we commend to thy gracious keeping, O Lord, all thy servants who have departed this life in thy faith and fear, beseeching thee, according to thy promises, to grant them refreshment, light and peace." [13]

"Hear us as we remember those who have died in the peace of Christ, both those who have confessed the faith and those whose faith is known to you alone, and grant us with them a share in your eternal kingdom." [14]

In the Common Worship funeral service,[15] the main place of praying for the person who has died is in the prayer of entrusting and commending. The prayers offered in the resources express our faith and hope in salvation, and in that context, put the person who has died into God's hands. Prayers for the individual are set in the context of praying for all the faithful dead. The actual prayer for the deceased in the prayer of commendation can be as simple as "we entrust N to your mercy", but sometimes a little more is requested:

"... So we commend N to your arms of mercy,
believing that, with sins forgiven,
he/she will share a place of happiness, light and peace
in the kingdom of your glory for ever."

Sometimes the prayers are not so much for the person who has died, but for ourselves, for instance, that God "will show us the path of life, and the fullness of joy in your presence."

Cocksworth makes a distinction between prayers at the funeral and prayers at the time of death, when more specific prayers may be appropriate. This is reflected in the prayers available for use when someone has just died, in which we pray:

.... That death may be for him/her
the gate to life and to eternal fellowship with you ...

... grant to him/her and to all who rest in Christ,
refreshment, light and peace ... [16]

---

[13] Archbishops' Council, *Common Worship*, p. 284
[14] Archbishops' Council, *Common Worship*, p. 285
[15] Archbishops' Council, *Pastoral Services*, pp 267, 373-376
[16] Common Worship: Pastoral Services, p. 234

Another prayer for use at the time of death sets out in more detail what we want God to do for the person who has just died:

> Into your hands, Lord,
> our faithful creator and most loving redeemer,
> we commend your child N,
> for *he/she* is yours in death as in life.
> In your great mercy
> fulfil in *him/her* the purpose of your love;
> gather *him/her* to yourself in gentleness and peace,
> that, rejoicing in the light and refreshment of your presence,
> *he/she* may enjoy the rest which you have prepared for your
> faithful servants;
> through Jesus Christ our Lord.[17]

The Report of the Archbishops' Commission on Christian Doctrine recognises a need to pray not just for those who have died in Christ, but for "the dead of all mankind, including those who have died in the practice of other religions, those who were indifferent, those who never came to the knowledge of Christ, those who lost their faith, and those who died in open rebellion against God"[18] and this prayer is recommended:

> O God of infinite mercy and justice, who hast made man in thine
> own image, and hated nothing that thou hast made, we rejoice in
> thy love for all creation and commend all men to thee, that in
> them thy will be done, in and through Jesus Christ our Lord.

And the Litany includes this prayer which asks that those whose faith is known only to God may also share in the eternal kingdom:

> Hear us as we remember
> those who have died in the peace of Christ,
> both those who have confessed the faith
> and those whose faith is known to you alone,
> and grant us with them a share in your eternal kingdom.[19]

---

[17] *Common Worship: Pastoral Services*, p. 375.
[18] Archbishops' Commission on Christian Doctrine, *Prayer and the Departed*, p.53
[19] *Common Worship*, p. 114

The Kontakion for the Departed is offered as a resource in *Pastoral Services*. This is an explicit prayer for the dead:

> Give rest, O Christ, to your servant with the saints:
> where sorrow and pain are no more,
> neither sighing, but life everlasting.[20]

It was already publicly available to the church in the first edition of the English Hymnal published in 1906. A request that it be sung at the funeral of Queen Victoria was denied, on the grounds that it was not in accord with the teachings of the Church of England.[21] It was used during the funerals of Prince Philip and Queen Elizabeth II, so attitudes have changed.

It has been traditional in some parts of the Anglican Church to hold a Eucharist on All Souls Day to remember those who have died, in which their names are read out weeks, months, years after their death. This has been incorporated into Common Worship liturgy.[22] Some churches may use some of the resources offered, particularly the Commemoration of the Faithful Departed,[23] in a Service of the Word rather than a Eucharist. The emphasis in these prayers is very much on praying for the *faithful* departed, in the company of the saints in light, that they may find peace and joy in the kingdom of God.

> Lord God, creator of all, ...
> According to your promises,
> may all who have died in the peace of Christ
> come with your saints to the joys of your kingdom,
> where there will be neither sorrow or pain,
> but life everlasting.
> **Alleluia. Amen**[24]

---

[20] *Common Worship: Pastoral Services*, p 232
[21] See Wikipedia entry on Kontakion: Kontakion - Wikipedia
[22] The Archbishops' Council, *Common Worship: Times and Seasons*, 2006, Church House Publishing, pp 561-572
[23] *Ibid.*, pp 570-571
[24] *Common Worship: Times and Seasons*, p 570

And

> Grant to us, Lord God,
> to trust you not for ourselves alone,
> but for those also whom we love
> and who are hidden from us by the shadow of death;
> that, as we believe your power to have raised our Lord Jesus
> Christ from the dead,
> so may we trust your love
> to give eternal life to all who believe in him; ...[25]

In the Order of Service for Remembrance Sunday,[26] the emphasis is on remembering the dead of war and praying for peace and for those who wish us harm. However, among the additional resources is a rare example of an Anglican prayer that more specifically prays for the dead:

> Almighty and eternal God,
> from whose love in Christ we cannot be parted,
> either by death or life:
> hear our prayers and thanksgivings for all whom we
> remember this day;
> fulfil in them the purpose of your love;
> and bring us all with them, to your eternal joy;
> through Jesus Christ our Lord.
> Amen[27]

The prayer asks God to "fulfil in them the purpose of your love", which is a fairly open prayer, but implies the possibility of post-mortem improvement. This prayer originates in the Official 1968 Order for Remembrance.[28]

The blessing recommended for services of Remembrance prays:

> God grant to the living grace,
> to the departed rest, ...

---

[25] Ibid

[26] Common Worship: Times and Seasons, pp 575-585

[27] Ibid., p 582

[28] The text of the 1968 service can be found in Brian Elliott, They Shall Grow not Old, pp 108-115

14

>   and to us and all God's servants,
>   life everlasting ...

and incorporates all the departed, not just those who were faithful.

Thus, the prayers published for use in many forms of worship in the Church of England do not all follow the Church's stated principles, and this is to be applauded. It might also be that attitudes have softened over time.

Another Slant

The Report of the Archbishops' Commission on Christian Doctrine recognises the contribution of psychical research and also cites some cases.[29]

The traditional theology of death and what happens next pretty much rules out further spiritual growth post mortem. However, psychic and spiritual insights suggest the possibility that our development does not cease at death. Helen Greaves received psychic communication from her friend Frances Banks, a former nun, who had died, setting out Frances' experience of the next life as a time of healing, where she was able to grow and to help others on their continuing spiritual journeys. If we accept this picture of life after death, it has implications for the way we pray for the dead.

Through Helen, Frances tells us that praying for the dead is really important. These prayers are like "a draught of healing water for the newly transmitted soul."[30] Martin Israel says that "prayer for the dead is a most important spiritual duty for a Christian."[31]

Traditional theology and liturgy are centred on the faithful dead. Greaves and Israel emphasise the need to pray for those whose lives were evil and who caused great harm. Israel, most of whose family were killed by the Nazis, talks about his own vocation to pray for deceased war criminals. "The evil ones of our earth should be prayed for in terms of healing, because until they are healed, we too will remain unhealed."[32] He advocates special prayer

---

[29] Archbishops' Commission on Christian Doctrine, *Prayer and the Departed*, Appendix 1, pp. 61-66
[30] Greaves, *Testimony of Light*, p. 65
[31] Israel, *The Communion of Saints*, p. 15
[32] Israel, *The Communion of Saints*, p. 16

groups "bringing the power of Christ into the dark places and remembering, in love, various classes of criminals and … those … who we find repulsive".[33] Greaves describes prayers for those in darkness as "the sending out of Light …, the deliberate formation of a prayer thought …, a moment of remembrance in a holy place, even the uttering of … names … commending them to Divine Mercy … all are helps towards the resurrection of those who dwell in darkness."[34]

It seems that the dead do need our prayers, despite Cocksworth's assertion that they don't. They need encouragement, recognition of existence and acknowledgment of their presence. They need light and love, just as we do.

Robert Crookall's analysis of communications apparently from the dead refers to various instances when the dead have pleaded for prayer.[35] Apparently, prayers from those who are still "in the body" are very important for souls who are stuck. And those recently deceased also "greatly benefit by the prayers of 'living' friends."[36] Crookall suggests that those who most need these prayers are those who made little moral or spiritual progress in their lives on earth.

The growth of interest in Near Death Experiences (NDEs)[37] has also altered and shaped the way people understand life after death. Raymond Moody coined the term in 1975. Bruce Greyson began studying NDEs in the late 1970s, trying to identify physiological explanations. The causes are still uncertain, but the experiences are found in all cultures and in all times. NDEs may happen at death or close to death. Accounts vary, but often describe separation from the body and travelling to another place where the person might encounter significant people. They then return to the body and surprisingly recover, with a renewed sense of life continuing beyond death,

---

[33] Israel, The communion of Saints, p. 17
[34] Greaves, *Testimony of Light*, p. 66
[35] Robert Crookall, *The Supreme Adventure*, Appendix IV, pp. 234 ff
[36] Robert Crookall, *The Supreme Adventure*, p. 64.
[37] See Raymond Moody, *Life After Life*, Bruce Greyson, *After*, Eben Alexander, *Proof of Heaven*. There are many websites about NDEs, for example NDERF Home Page and IANDS - the most reliable source of information on NDEs. There are also YouTube channels: Jeff Mara and Next Level Soul are two channels which are highly regarded.

and a clearer sense of their own purpose in this life. Accounts also suggest that a person who has "died" in this way, can respond to the prayers or requests of loved ones to return. This was the experience of neurosurgeon Dr Eben Alexander who contracted meningoencephalitis, with a 2% chance of survival. He experienced a beautiful land and a conversation with God, until his son called him back. The work on NDEs doesn't generally refer to people on earth praying for those who have passed over and the effect of those prayers, but it reinforces an understanding of the afterlife and the continuation of some part of the human consciousness which continues to grow.

Fr Nathan Castle OP, a Catholic priest, has a special vocation to pray for those who have died suddenly or violently, helping them to cross over into the afterlife. He had a practice of handing over his consciousness to God as he settled for sleep. He started to have dreams about people who had died in terrible circumstances, and were stuck. Fr Nathan learnt how to help them through understanding their situation and praying for them. According to the interview with Donna Rebadow found on his website,[38] he has helped nearly 400 people move on. He is clear that this work is guided by the Holy Spirit and that Guardian Angels are also involved in helping the individuals and preparing them for the work with Fr Nathan.

These witnesses have learnt about the importance of praying for the dead through their own experience or research. Prayer can help those who have died move on or come to terms with their death and previous life.

The Theological Approach Taken in this Book of Prayers

Calling this booklet "Praying for the Dead" is a misnomer, a shorthand for a larger truth. To talk of "the dead", implies that they are no more. Certainly they are no more with us in physical form, but those who are no longer physically present here on earth are still living, in a different way, on another plane, in another dimension. And they may not be too far away from us.

Some talk of those who have "passed over" into the next life. Celebrants and funeral directors no longer talk of the deceased as dead, but as "passed",

---

[38] Father Nathan Castle, O.P. (nathan-castle.com)

which can feel like a euphemism. The reality for those who are grieving is that their loved one is no longer present to them as they once were, and they need to let go and adjust to new circumstances. It is often hard for them to accept that the loved one is now living a new life when they would rather have them present here and now. For these relatives, they need to hear about death as well as the Christian hope of resurrection. For those who pray, the focus is on those who have made the transition into the next life, but still need our prayers and encouragement.

We are often asked to pray for others, friends and neighbours, and the wider community, especially in times of illness or trouble, and those who pray do that gladly. We may ask others to pray for us. There is a mutuality about prayer. In prayer, we hold the other in the light, in love, before God, telling God about the illness or trouble, and asking for assistance according to the will of God. And when we pray, we too are held in that light and love. Just as we pray for those who are living on earth, we can be drawn to pray for those who are living the next life and those who are stuck between. Sometimes, we might address the loved one directly, "God bless you Joan", and rejoice in the blessing they bring us.

When we pray for those who have died, we hold them in God's light and love. We probably don't know what they need, but we put them into God's hands, longing for them to thrive and grow and flourish in love. It may be that they need to accept their transition; it may be that they need to acknowledge and integrate the lives they led here on earth; it may be they need to accept greater truths. And so we give them to God. Those who passed over suddenly or in violence or in great distress may have particular need for prayer. And so we give them to God. Those whose lives on earth were difficult or who caused great harm to others may also need prayer. And so we give them to God.

This is perhaps the most controversial aspect of the prayers proposed here, that we pray for those whose lives were unwholesome and whose deeds were evil, those who did not die in the faith of Christ. They may not be the easiest of people to pray for while they live on earth, and this can be especially true when they have moved on. When we pray for them, we are asking for light to shine in the deep darkness of their lives and personalities. They are God's children, made by a loving God, and we long for that love to make a difference.

There is potential danger in engaging with things of the spirit. Not everything in the world beyond is friendly or benign. When we pray for those who have passed over, we need protection from anything that might hurt or harm us.   When we are open to the world of spirit we can encounter unhealthy and unhelpful forces. Suitable prayers of protection are included.

The prayers are drawn from many sources. We hope that groups and individuals called to this work of prayer will find the suggested order and format helpful.   It is an informal way of praying. At each section, group members are encouraged to talk briefly about the causes and persons on their minds, and to select one of the suggested prayers to draw their concerns together before God, or use their own words. The chat is as important a part of the process as the recommended prayers themselves. It might be helpful to have a leader to guide the process, but it doesn't need to be the same person every time, and it doesn't need to be a qualified minister. The leader should help everyone to contribute as they wish.

Bibliography

Eben Alexander, *Proof of Heaven: A Neurosurgeon's Journey into the Afterlife*, 2012.

Nathan G Castle, *Afterlife, Interrupted: Helping Stuck Souls Cross Over* (Books 1 and 2),

Archbishops' Council, *Common Worship: Services and Prayers for the Church of England*, 2000, Church House Publishing

The Archbishops' Council, *Common Worship,* 2000, Church House Publishing

The Archbishops' Council, *Common Worship: Pastoral Services,* 2000, Church House Publishing

The Archbishops' Council, *Common Worship: Times and Seasons*, 2006, Church House Publishing

Archbishops' Commission on Christian Doctrine, *Prayer and the Departed*, 1971, SPCK

Catechism of the Catholic Church, 1994, Geoffrey Chapman, London.

Christopher Cocksworth, *Prayer and the Departed*, 1997, Grove Books Worship Series 142

Robert Crookall, *The Supreme Adventure: Analyses of Psychic communications*, 1961, James Clarke & Co Ltd

Brian Elliott, *They Shall Grow Not Old: Liturgies for Remembrance*, 2006, Canterbury Press.

Helen Greaves, *Testimony of Light*, 1969, CFPSS

Bruce Greyson, *After: A Doctor Explores What Near-Death Experiences Reveal about Life and Beyond*, 2021

Michael S Heiser, *The Unseen Realm*, 2015, Lexham Press

Martin Israel, *The Communion of Saints*, 1980, CFPSS

Raymond Moody, *Life After Life*, 1975.

NT Wright, *For All the Saints? Remembering the Christian Departed*, 2003, SPCK

Praying for the Dead : A Form of Prayers

The pattern and prayers offered here are not intended as a formal liturgy, but as a resource that may be helpful to those who meet to pray for those who have died. Use what is helpful. Ignore what is not. Take time in each section to name and talk about those who are on your hearts, and commend them into the hands of our Living Lord, perhaps using one of the prayers suggested or voicing your own prayers.

OPENING PRAYERS

One of these opening prayers may be said:
We meet in the presence of God
who knows our needs,
hears our cries,
feels our pain,
and heals our wounds.[1]

We stand before the throne of God
with countless crowds
from every nation and race, tribe and language.
Blessing and glory and wisdom,
thanksgiving and honour, power and might
be to our God for ever and ever. Amen[2]

Jesus Christ is the light of the world:
a light no darkness can quench.
Stay with us, Lord, for it is evening:
and the day is almost over.
Even the darkness is not dark for you:
and the night shines like the day.
Let your light scatter the darkness:
and fill your church with your glory.[3]

---

[1] *New Patterns for Worship*, A34
[2] *New Patterns for Worship*, A24
[3] *New Patterns of Worship*, A18

BIBLE READING

A short Bible reading may help to inform our prayers. You might like to use one of these,[4] or another:

The Lord is my light and my salvation; whom then shall I fear? (Psalm 27:1)

The Lord Jesus says: Today you will be with me in Paradise. (Luke 23:43)

Do not let your hearts be troubled. Believe in God, believe also in me. In my Father's house there are many dwelling places. If it were not so, would I have told you that I go to prepare a place for you? And if I go and prepare a place for you, I will come again and will take you to myself, so that where I am, there you may be also. (John 14:1-3)

I desire that those also, whom you have given me, may be with me where I am, to see my glory. (John 17:24)

We do not live to ourselves, and we do not die to ourselves. If we live, we live to the Lord, and if we die, we die to the Lord; so then, whether we live or whether we die, we are the Lord's. For to this end Christ died and lived again, so that he might be Lord of both the dead and the living. (Romans 14:7-9)

But in fact Christ has been raised from the dead, the first fruits of those who have died. For since death came through a human being, the resurrection of the dead has also come through a human being; for as all die in Adam, so all will be made alive in Christ. (1 Corinthians 15:20-22)

Christ died and lived again, so that he might be Lord of both the dead and the living. (Romans 14:9)

Other possibilities might include: Psalm 121, Romans 8:35-39, 1 Corinthians 15:51-57, Revelation 21:1-4, Revelation 22:1-5

PRAYER OF PROTECTION

When we pray for the dead who may be in dark places, there is a chance that we become open to dark influences which might prey upon us and wish us harm. It is well, therefore, to pray our good Lord to guard us and guide us, protect us and defend us. One of these prayers may be helpful.

---

[4] The verses here are taken from the New Revised Standard Version Anglicized edition, 1995.

22

Visit, Lord, we pray, this place
and drive far from it all the snares of the enemy.
Let your holy angels dwell here to keep us in peace,
and may your blessing be upon it evermore;
through Jesus Christ our Lord. Amen[5]

May the cross of the Son of God,
which is mightier than all the hosts of Satan
and more glorious than all the hosts of heaven,
abide with us in our going out and in our coming in.
By day and by night, at morning and at evening,
at all times and in all places
may it protect and defend us.
From the wrath of evildoers, from the assaults of evil spirits,
from foes visible and invisible, from the snares of the devil,
from all the passions that beguile the soul and body:
may it guard, protect and deliver us. Amen[6]

Thou, who art the eternal protection and salvation of our souls,
arm us, we entreat Thee, with the helmet of hope,
and the shield of Thy invincible defence;
that so, helped by Thee in the straits of our necessities,
we may be filled with joy and gladness with those who love Thee,
through Jesus Christ our Lord.[7]

I bind unto myself today
The power of God to hold and lead,
His eye to watch, His might to stay,
His ear to hearken to my need.
The wisdom of my God to teach,
His hand to guide, His shield to ward;
The word of God to give me speech,
His heavenly host to be my guard.

---

[5] *Common Worship Pastoral Services*, p. 96
[6] *Common Worship Pastoral Services*, p. 96, no. 1, adapted
[7] From Sarum Breviary, in Elizabeth Goudge, *A Diary of Prayer*, p. 28

Christ be with me, Christ within me,
Christ behind me, Christ before me,
Christ beside me, Christ to win me,
Christ to comfort and restore me.
Christ beneath me, Christ above me,
Christ in quiet, Christ in danger,
Christ in hearts of all that love me,
Christ in mouth of friend and stranger.[8]

THANKSGIVING FOR THE LIVES OF LOVED ONES

We pray for our own loved ones at their anniversaries and special occasions, in gratitude and tender memory. When we have named them, one of these prayers may express what we desire for them:

Father of all,
we pray to you for those whom we love but see no longer.
We thank you
for the peace and light you bestow upon them;
in your loving wisdom and almighty power
continue to work in them
the good purpose of your perfect will,
through Jesus Christ our Lord. Amen[9]

Lord of all, we praise you
for all who have entered into their rest
and reached the promised land where you are seen face to face.
Give us grace to follow in their footsteps
as they followed in the way of your Son.
Thank you for the memory of those you have called to yourself;
by each memory, turn our hearts from things seen to things unseen,
and lead us till we come to the eternal rest
you have prepared for your people,
through Jesus Christ our Lord. Amen.[10]

---

[8] St Patrick's Breastplate
[9] *A New Zealand Prayer Book*, p 858, no 13
[10] *Common Worship Pastoral Prayers*, p. 351, no. 18

Father of all, we commend to thy mercy
all our friends who have died.
Grant them more light
and further opportunities for progress in the knowledge of thee.
If it be possible, may they pray for us as we do now for them.
Unite us in the communion of Saints and the fellowship of the Holy Spirit,
for Jesus' sake. Amen[11]

THOSE WHO HAVE DIED

We pray for those who have died, seeking the help of the saints and angels as they make the transition into new life and their continued growth in faith and hope and love. Pray especially for those who have died in tragic circumstances – violence, war, terrorism, famine, disaster. There are so many – focus on those you feel called to pray for. May God's light shine in the darkness.

> Unto thy tender and searching compassion, O Lord,
> do we commit all those who have died with little faith and few good deeds;
> those who were blinded to thy glory by our unfaithfulness;
> and all who have never known Thy gospel.
> Grant that these,
> when they awaken to thy presence and see thee as thou art,
> may know the greatness of thy mercy;
> through Jesus Christ our Lord.[12]

> O Father of all,
> we pray to Thee for those whom we love, but see no longer.
> Grant them Thy peace; let light perpetual shine upon them;
> and in Thy loving wisdom and almighty power
> work in them the good purpose of Thy perfect will;
> through Jesus Christ our Lord.[13]

---

[11] W R Matthews, in *The Oxford Book of Prayer*, no. 546
[12] From *New Every Morning*, reprinted in Elizabeth Goudge, *A Diary of Prayer*, p. 245.
[13] The Order for the Burial of the Dead, *Book of Common Prayer* 1928

Welcome, Lord, into your calm and peaceful kingdom
those who, out of this present life, have departed to be with you;
grant them rest and a place with the spirits of the just;
and give them the life that knows not age,
the reward that passes not away,
through Jesus Christ our Lord. Amen[14]

Hasten to meet them, Angels of the Lord,
Receiving their souls and offering them in the sight of the Most High.
May Christ who called you take you to himself
And may the angels lead you to Abraham's bosom.
Eternal rest grant unto them, Lord,
And let perpetual light shine upon them.[15]

THOSE WHO DID EVIL

We pray regularly and systematically for those who have done great evil in the world. Ask God to lead you to those for whom you should pray – people you read about in newspapers or other media, people you learn about from other sources. Pray that the power of the light of Christ may shine in their darkness and that they might find healing.

God, creator and redeemer of all,
grant to the souls of the departed
forgiveness for all their sins,
light in their darkness,
love to overcome fear and hatred,
and peace in their turmoil;
through Jesus Christ who emptied himself
that all might find freedom in him. Amen[16]

---

[14] St Ignatius of Loyola, in Angela Ashwin, *A Book of a Thousand Prayers*, no. 582
[15] Roman Liturgy for the dying, in Eamon Duffy (ed), *The Heart in Pilgrimage*, p. 161
[16] MMG

MEMORIES IGNITED

As you pray for those who have done great harm in the world, your prayers may trigger for you memories of hurt you have endured. Hold these memories before our gracious God, and let God's light and love flow into these dark places. You may want to do this later on your own. Or you may signal to the group "our prayers have triggered something for me here" – you don't need to go into details if you don't want to. Ask the group to hold you in prayer.

> God of all mercies, hold *me/us/N* in your loving care.
> Hold *us*, heal *us*, restore and renew *us*.
> Let your light shine here in the dark places of *our* hearts
> and in the hearts of those who have caused *us* harm.
> May your peace reign as we entrust our memories to you,
> through Jesus Christ, our Lord and Saviour.[17]

PRAYING FOR OURSELVES

Having prayed for others who have died, we seek God's light in our own lives here on earth. One of these prayers may be helpful here.

> God and Father of our Lord Jesus Christ,
> bring us to the dwelling
> which your Son is preparing for all who love you.
> Give us the will each day to live in life eternal.
> Let our citizenship be in heaven
> with the whole company of the redeemed
> and with countless angels,
> praising, worshipping and adoring him
> who sits upon the throne for ever and ever. Amen[18]

---

[17] MMG
[18] *New Patterns of Worship*, J34

Living God,
you have lit the day with the sun's light
and the midnight with shining stars.
Lighten our hearts with the bright beams
of the Sun of Righteousness
risen with healing in his wings,
Jesus Christ our Lord.
And so preserve us in the doing of your will,
that at the last we may shine as the stars for ever;
through the same Jesus Christ our Lord. Amen.[19]

Eternal God, our maker and defender,
grant us, with all the faithful departed,
the sure benefits of your Son's saving passion and glorious
resurrection
that, in the last day, when you gather up all things in Christ,
we may with them enjoy the fullness of your promises;
through Jesus Christ our Lord. Amen[20]

Bring us, O Lord God, at the last awakening
into the house and gate of heaven,
to enter into that gate and dwell in that house,
where there shall be no darkness nor dazzling, but one equal light;
no noise nor silence, but one equal music;
no fears nor hopes, but an equal possession;
no ends nor beginnings, but one equal eternity;
in the habitations of Thy majesty and Thy glory, world without
end.[21]

---

[19] *Common Worship Pastoral Prayers*, p. 364, no. 56
[20] SSF, *Celebrating Common Prayer* Pocket Edition, p. 322.
[21] John Donne (1573-1631)

CLOSING PRAYERS

Now we are bringing all our prayers together. One of these prayers might suffice:

Eternal rest grant them, O Lord,
and let light perpetual shine upon them.
Hear us, O merciful Father,
as we remember in love
those whom we have placed into your hands.
Acknowledge, we pray, the sheep of your own fold,
lambs of your own flock,
sinners of your own redeeming.
Enfold them in the arms of your mercy,
in the blessed rest of everlasting peace,
and in the glorious company of the saints in light. Amen[22]

The Lord's Prayer

You can end your time of prayer with one of these blessing prayers:

May Christ,
who out of defeat brings new hope and a new future,
fill us with his new life;
and may God's blessing rest on us
and on those for whom we have prayed, always. Amen[23]

May God give us his comfort and his peace,
his light and his joy,
in this world and the next;
and may God's blessing rest on us
and on those for whom we have prayed, always. Amen[24]

---

[22] *Common Worship Times and Seasons*, p. 571.
[23] Adapted from *New Patterns of Worship*, J85
[24] Adapted from *New Patterns of Worship*, J112

May the eternal God
bless and keep us, guard our bodies,
save our souls and bring us safe to the heavenly country,
our eternal home,
where Father, Son, and Holy Spirit reign,
one God for ever and ever. Amen[25]

And now to him who is able to keep us from falling,
and lift us from the dark valley of despair
to the bright mountain of hope,
from the midnight of desperation
to the daybreak of joy;
to him be power and authority, for ever and ever. Amen[26]

OTHER USEFUL PRAYERS

These wonderful prayers might be useful on occasion:

Give rest, O Christ, to your servant with the saints:
where sorrow and pain are no more;
neither sighing, but life everlasting.
You only art immortal, the creator and maker of all:
and we are mortal formed from the dust of the earth,
and unto earth shall we return:
for so you ordained when you created me, saying:
"Dust you art und to dust you shall return."
All of us go down to the dust;
and weeping at the grave we make our song:
Alleluia, alleluia, alleluia.[27]

---

[25] *Common Worship Pastoral Services*, p.378, no. 84
[26] *Common Worship Pastoral Services*, p. 377, no. 80
[27] Russian Kontakion for the Dead

O Lord Jesus, who knowest them that are thine;
When thou rewardest thy servants the prophets,
remember we beseech thee, for good
those who have taught us, counselled us, guided us,
and in that day show them mercy:
When thou rewardest the saints,
remember, we beseech thee, for good
those who have surrounded us with holy influences,
borne with us, forgiven us, sacrificed themselves for us, loved us,
and in that day show them mercy;
Nor forget any, nor forget us, but in that day show us mercy,
O Lord, thou lover of souls.[27]

My Lord God, even now I accept at your hands, cheerfully and
willingly,
with all its anxieties, pains and sufferings,
whatever kind of death it shall please you to make mine. Amen[28]

Carry us, Christ, on your Cross,
which is salvation to the wanderer,
rest for the wearied,
and in which alone is life for those who die.[29]

Bibliography: Source of Prayers and Copyright Holders

George Appleton (general editor), *The Oxford Book of Prayer*, Oxford University
Press, 1985

The Archbishops Council of the Church of England:

Common Worship: Services and Prayers for the Church of England, 2000

Common Worship: Pastoral Services, 2000

Common Worship: Times & Seasons, 2006

Patterns for Worship, 1995

---

[28] Christina Rossetti, in Elizabeth Goudge, *A Diary of Prayer*, p. 240
[29] Eamon Duffy (ed), *The Heart in Pilgrimage*, p. 164.
[30] St Ambrose, in Eamon Duffy (ed), *The Heart in Pilgrimage*, p. 165

Cambridge University Press, *The Prayer Book as proposed in 1928*

The Church of the Province of New Zealand, *A New Zealand Prayer Book,* Collins, 1989

Eamon Duffy (ed), *The Heart in Pilgrimage*, Bloomsbury, 2013

Elizabeth Goudge, *A Diary of Prayer*, Hodder and Stoughton, 1966

The Society of St Francis (SSF), *Celebrating Common Prayer*, pocket edition, 2002

Note on Copyright

Churches Fellowship for Psychical and Spiritual Studies (CFPSS)

Office 8, The Creative Suite, Mill 3, Pleasley Vale Business Park, Mansfield, Notts., G19 8RL

Telephone: 01623 812206
gensec@churchesfellowship.co.uk

About the Churches Fellowship...

The CFPSS exists to promote the study of psychical and spiritual experience within a Christian context. Founded in 1953 by a group of clergy and lay people on an ecumenical basis, it continues to serve the churches and its individual members who come from many and varied backgrounds.

Some have sought help from the Fellowship's extensive knowledge, at significant points in life where there may have been spontaneous gifts of the Spirit, the pain of bereavement or simply a vocation to a spiritual life through psychic encounter. Many bring a wisdom and depth of vision to enrich the understanding of others.

The Fellowship takes an understanding view of psychic sensitivity which many people experience quite naturally in their lives, perhaps through an unsought telepathic communication. Some seem to have a greater awareness of this dimension than others and in some it is more refined. There is a gentle call on members to relate this to a fuller Christian life in which the psychic may find consecration.

**The Churches Fellowship
for Psychical and Spiritual Studies**

Office 8, the Creative Suite
Mill 3, Pleasley Vale Business Park
Mansfield, Notts., NG19 8RL

Tel 01623 812 206

(Founder Lt-Col. Reginald M. Lester FJI)

Registered Charity No 233778

Email: gensec@churchesfellowship.co.uk
Website: www.churchesfellowship.co.uk

**Patrons include the Rt Revd Dr Rowan Williams and the
Rt Revd Richard Chartres**

More resources about death and praying for the dead:

Other books and booklets from the Churches Fellowship for Psychical and Spiritual Studies

Books

Spiritualism: The 1939 Report to the Archbishop of Canterbury

Angels in Dark Places	Beryl Statham
One Witness	Barbara Bunce
They Need No Candle	E J Cotton

Booklets:

About Bereavement	Revd Dr Martin Israel
About Death	Revd Dr Martin Israel (& others)
About Prayer	Revd Dr Martin Israel (& others)
And the Life of the World to Come	Revd Dr Martin Israel
The Intermediate Dimension	Revd Dr Martin Israel
The Communion of Saints	Revd Dr Martin Israel
Horizons of Perception	Barbara Bunce

Members also have access to the CFPSS library and collection
of audio recordings